USED

REJECTED

DR. CORTEZ D. SIMS

QUALIFIED,

BUT NOT PREFERRED!

A cost for being yourself

DAMAGED

SCARRED

OVERLOOKED

UNDER ESTIMATED

ABAND

FOREWORD BY **DARRYL L. RIVERS**
AUTHOR OF "LEARNING TO LOVE YOUR MONDAYS"

Qualified, But Not Preferred! A Cost for Being Yourself

Published by Dr. Cortez D. Sims, Plus More Publishing
drcortezsims@gmail.com

Distribution by Kindle Direct Publishing Amazon.com Printed in the United States of America

Library of Congress cataloged the original edition as follows:
Qualified, But Not Preferred! A cost for being yourself!
Application: Psychology/Developmental/ Lifespan Development

Cover design Burn Graphics & Dr. Cortez D. Sims
Photography J & K Photography

Special Thanks to the guest editors:

ISBN 978-0-9978642-3-6

DEDICATIONS
In Memory of

Woodroe "Popps" Sims

Jack C. "Lil Jack" Hall

Pastor Terrance "Chat" Chatman

Darryl "DC Groove" Bulluck

Derwin "DA Maestro" Davis

Tracey Anita "Ms. Bass" Baker

Roderick "Hot Rod" Gibson

The servants that have modeled the true
meaning of being *True Soldiers* in my life.
Rest in Heaven.
Well, done God's good and faithful servants!
Matthew 25:21 NLT

TABLE OF
CONTENTS

TABLE OF
CONTENTS

FOREWORD

I can vividly recall multiple situations when I was called upon to conduct a task that I believed myself to be vastly under-equipped to perform. Yet, for some reason, there I was in a position of expectation from others, while my inward position was "man, this is going to be embarrassing." One that comes to mind is from my days as an Aviation Ordnanceman in the United States Navy in the 1990s. I had just made "rank," (E-4, Non-Commissioned Officer) and I was immediately given charge of six other ordnancemen while conducting operations in the Persian Gulf. I knew all there was to know to do the job technically, yet I had limited operational experience leading a team when the stakes were high. I was twenty-one years old, I had lots of ambition, zeal, and technical knowledge, but little leadership experience. Yes, I was a popular kid in high school, and my neighborhood peers knew about me and respected me because I was a teenage kid that went on dates with older women. It was great to have all that attention and admiration from my friends. It was also great to not have their safety and ultimately their lives dependent on my leadership decisions. Once I began the leadership tasks my country placed on my shoulders, I learned many things about myself. The most important was that I could be a pretty good leader, despite the many pressures the flight deck of an aircraft carrier can present. Yet the more grounded I became, the more I realized I was not preferred. Then I had the opportunity to visit Haifa, Israel. I took a bus ride to Jerusalem. My visit to Jerusalem changed the trajectory of my leadership. Once my focus became different, my view of systematic opposition became clear. When our focus is more defined, so is any and everything that attempts to distort that focus.

We can find ourselves not recognizing other's disdain for not only our ability to do what needs to be done but most importantly, our selection to do what must be done when we have doubts about our ability or our selection. BUT MY GOD, when we know we are qualified inwardly and outwardly, things take on a completely different color. When the voices of men direct destruction toward your journey and provide themselves as a mountain in the way, please know if you are qualified to tackle the task, you are qualified to climb the mountains in front of the task. And yes, I know mountains do not get tired. This is why the truths put to these pages from Dr. Cortez Sims are so vital to our task. The mountains of men can be a place of exhaustion while we climb, or a resting place in between each push toward our ultimate goals. Mental exhaustion usually precedes the actions of our hearts that fuel our exit to our most important task. The examples provided in this book will open the mental doors to allow us to get better and not bitter, along with the correct heart position to remain Godly focused on the mission and not the push of mankind that plots to pull us apart from it.

As a military veteran and retired law enforcement professional, I have had my share of mountains, but not from the adversarial forces that were expected. Unfortunately, many of my mountains wore the same uniform as I. I've tested in the top elements of personnel and was passed up for promotion on a few occasions. I've been promoted and demoted. I've been denied where the less qualified and reputable were positioned to thrive. I've been advised to quit by my mountains and those closest to me. Yet through it all, my encouraging brother and friend, Dr. Sims, stood by me and walked with me. We co-labored in ministry endeavors and grew great connections. I have had a front-row seat to him and his mountains, and I am sure you will be thoroughly encouraged and equipped to live out your qualifications despite the preferences of men.

Darryl L. Rivers
National Speaker/Trainer and Founder/Owner "The L.E.A.D. Company"

INTRODUCTION

It is not uncommon for anyone to think or dare to believe that all things should be measured fairly. Unfortunately, "fair" is not the most exciting word to announce because of the perspective you may weigh against what you may interpret. In fact, the origin of a concept can have its prejudices of acceptance due to the unfamiliar or even ignorance of one's preconception of that concept. In other words, the originality of a thing can be naturally accepted before opinions, judgments, or stereotypes are even formed. Many times, it is categorized based upon a person's past or background that is ostracized despite its pure innocence. Therefore, when one is born, the child is quickly placed in the boundaries of a family war of where it goes, identification, gender, complexion, and bodily features.

Qualified, But Not Preferred shares a variety of life experiences in one's personal pains of rejection, discrimination, and stereotypes with many who have developed difficulties receiving what they did not deserve, without having any control over being a natural human being with individual qualities, morals, and standards. Today, we hear several stories and even view numerous films on fair treatment or intentional unfair treatment. It hurts my heart to see the effects of this behavior in facets beyond personal relationships, yet also throughout public relationships in this lifetime. It simply exposes the "chosen" from the "neglect" in true character. Many times, we're not even aware of the biases we perform and reflect on others. Many feel that if I spend time in my "truths," then at least I am honest with myself in my own perceptions, and not a part of the crowd's perceptions of a concept. The human race automatically has a diversion of self-truths, facts, principles, and their limited practicums. In some instances, it can be interpreted as ignorance to the knowledge of one's reality.

Chapter One

Qualifications

Why is it so important to qualify? Qualifications are noted on
the world wide web to mean a quality or accomplishment that
makes someone suitable for a particular job, activity or being
eligible. In the beginning stages of our lives as newborns and
infants through the adolescent stage of growth, we, as humans,
are silently becoming established immediately following our
delivery date. Identification gradually takes formation outwardly
in the circle of the mother, physicians and potential witnesses.
Race, gender and bodily features begin to unfold to the
audience in a forty-eight-hour classification category with one's
identity. Now, we're in the trusted hands of vital records to be
filed as an innocent gift from God to an unknown world. This
world was created by an unseen creator having the ability to
form such a science project that generates countless arguments
before mankind can grasp an understanding of its own
existence. A couple of years later, the child is introduced to
more human beings with names and features who subsequently
introduce them to other children in an environment called
"daycare school."

Based on the background of every parent or guardian, the same process of meeting the unfamiliar faces along with the ones at home grabs the cognitive attention of the child to the entire setting.

Now, the child is coupled with circles and circles of children with no understanding of cultural biases, backgrounds, or silent prejudices just to name a few politically. In this weekly or daily scheduled setting, they are introduced to learn colors, shapes, numbers, names, self- clothing, body language, restroom training, resting and nap periods, and meal differentials, snacks and all the full course meals offered. These all become the requirements it takes to operate as a growing human being in the adolescent years. Within a two to three-year period, the child is now graded on his daily performance.

This report is measured based on the retention of all the lessons taught and presented to him. It is also a time period when individual personality begins to find its way for further identification. This personality now defines the name, age, parents, household support, and the family upbringing and culture. This is the time when leaders are identified as the "true leaders versus the baby sitters" from the home front. This change of responsibility from parental guardian to teacher guides the child into the beginning of self-sufficiency of his responses to situations. In fact, the child segues into learning to share, pick, report, receive and earn mode. But now the facilitators of this process are weighing on the hired leaders with the burden of the agreement of all being treated "equally." Unfortunately, somewhere between daycare and home, many of us have experienced our first devastation when promised rewards and incentives. They were selected by votes, biases, differences, being the favorite people, or some other criteria, to share and to receive these awards. It is no wonder that confusion can develop early in the life of an infant's development and mindset, even in these early years.

Chapter Two
Doing What I Do....

As a counselor and life coach, I humbly acquired permission to share this young individual's life testimony anonymously. I must admit their story had disrupted my emotional and mental stability. Over twenty years of professional and volunteer practice I was not ready, nor was I prepared to hear their narrative as I have treated past clients. Consequently, their narrative impacted me and transferred my heart and soul to the point of empathizing with the emotional, mental, and informative need to share the experience as it relates to any of us that may read this book. The perspective of this young adult's experiences placed me in an open field to consider the silent tyranny many humans face in many diversified positions after becoming the exception to the rules. As a people, we commonly use words such as rejection, misjudged, overlooked, oversight, and dispensable after the state of inclusion is over. In fact, no one could ever measure how devastating that three-second decision towards someone's worth could alter the shaping of their future. What could be of very minimal impact to one who could potentially impute a level of misery to others, subsequently passed on to the thousands of people they will encounter because of the inconsiderate notion.

What's so ironic about this young person's narrative is that they're not the only human being who has experienced being qualified but not preferred. As I ponder on the one-on-one interviews we had, I realize now that our world is full of selfish gain and the lack of humility for human uniqueness. Therefore, disqualifications have become a power, a power that is prompted as a motivator to push what we call quality separate from generic as if both entities cannot perform quality assurance. This position of judgment is often espoused by an influential person who enriched notoriety. From the gains of a louder voice, charisma, and an audience that agrees to normally have only one outlook on a matter, and now this sudden experience impacts the inner being. It is also exercised in the audiences reflecting people who are taken away, enchanted, by this type of leadership.

Respectfully, I decided to listen thoroughly to the disgust and shame as they related their current position. They were a single parent, after years of being married, God-fearing, and educated. They had been blessed by having both mother and father figures, bringing up two children in harmony as much as possible, totally uncommon in today's circumstances. Truthfully, I am having an onerous time recording this narrative of truths, because everyone has lived or is currently facing this growing pain. There's nothing perfect about humans, but there are definitely humans that have a perfect truth originally created in the spirit by love.

Chapter Three

Caught Me Off Guard

Here I am, journaling the heartfelt words from this individual's mouth describing their past events. I instantly begin to memorize several authentic and relevant stories that I can relate to hearing, but nothing like this. Their conversation was captivating, without a doubt. Surprisingly, they started off by saying, "It was good that my life went this way. I am a better-polished individual for all I had been through and more." The conversation continued, revealing their recovery from the injuries of infidelity, manipulation, foolishness, and deception, just because their ex-spouse preferred another lifestyle outside of theirs. They said, "I was head-over-heels in love, but very naive to who they were in reality." Their story continued, "After leaving my family, ignoring the rumors at church, taking their child as my biological own, working two to three jobs for over seven years of faithfulness, always longing for their approval and happiness, I came to accept that I was a great spouse, parent, and leader, but not good enough in my partner's eyes to be eligible for a promising future.But the years of infidelity and disrespect were not acceptable anymore. I was naive, then a fool to forgive this toxic behavior over and over again.

Over, over and over again...then again. I began to not even recognize myself. At this point, I was losing my own identity." This self-revelation led to years of counseling and studying other surviving relationships to become my best with the help of two willing, dedicated, and determined coupled individuals.

The individual also said, "I can possibly be very dynamic in my relationship, but it would STILL not be enough. So, I lost myself. I lost time. I lost countless opportunities, yet I never qualified to be an exceptional companion in the eyes of my mate. Therefore, I had no other choice but to divorce that which was never mine wholeheartedly. I thought as long as I was the breadwinner, provider, trustworthy, exercised integrity, was favorable to God as well as people, a producer and a guarantee to show the love I was qualified." This individual's plight wasn't just the ordinary hurt we often hear in an abusive relationship. Their tone broadcast something much deeper than just this traumatic event. They verbally screamed, "Now I see what some innocent men and women go through. You give your devoted commitment and introduce them to family and friends for years, as the great spouse you thought you were. Being faithful, devoted, making them feel and seen as being number one; this was an advantage they had over me that only others can see. Just the simple things that people who are in love do without any regard."

This subject matter has become a common discussion among the tables, bars, taverns, television, big-screen films, and more for decades at a time. There is still blindness to it all, enabling the binding of the cycles of agony.

It personally takes me back to the dating process, with someone who has a high interest in courting for potential marriage while learning about their "opponent" in the process. In my professional opinion, I believe dating and courting are temporary moments of learning yourself. Yes, ourselves! And this continues for as long as we tend to shift our qualitative judgment on who and what to look for in a great mate during the thirty, sixty, and ninety-day periods. With no consideration or sensitivity to the candidate's background, experiences, philosophy, spiritual beliefs, and moral character, we forget that these are the true qualitative factors of what we should be considering in all relationships. This will instantly bring compliments or what I call "the rainbow flags" to question during the evaluation and assessment period. It is not by happenstance that in due time, slowly or quickly, your needed information will become indicators to guide one to their next set of decisions in a forward movement.

Childhood Blues

As I continued to record this individual's narrative, they began to reflect on their childhood disqualifying moments they'd experienced. Frankly, I did not understand what they meant, not their purpose, while sharing all of the sensitive moments. They began to share their kindergarten class experiences, excelling in reading comprehension, vocabulary, colors, and additional topics of learning at that time. There's one problem that became very noticeable and that was their ability to speak. They had acquired a speech impediment by mocking an uncle in a company of cousins whenever they would visit the extended family.

THIS EXPERIENCE CHANGED EVERYTHING! This impediment became the cliff that started several traumatic events of rejection, exclusiveness, desolation, resentment, and bitterness beyond their early development. Imagine this position when you're introducing your child to people. WOW! You know that parental posture, when the parent excitedly introduces their child/children to people and wants the child to say their name, and then repeat the other party's name, and your child merely stares because of the pressure to pronounce the name. The stuttering is so oppressing. The expressions and reactions from your parent's circle create such a silent, embarrassing moment. I can feel the strong emotion of this individual, although this occurred all the way back during their childhood. OMG! The can of worms has been opened.

They began to reflect on the early childhood classroom, having weekly presentations and assignments to speak as well as the grueling hard work at home in front of the parents in the bathroom mirror. This child became extremely, routinely nervous the night before each performance, because they were full of anxiousness and anxiety that they wanted to share from their heart, but couldn't. Yet the crucial stuttering would overshadow the words being said, later resulting in their classroom friends laughing all day and almost every day. Even the teacher would become frustrated with them holding up the class until their words eventually flustered out of their mouth. The child would listen to the neighboring teachers as they walked to the conjoined classrooms to collaborate on projects. They would pick other kids away, around and behind him, choosing any other child than the main one. It was quite embarrassing. This issue began to spread to their peers, faculty, and staff.

This embarrassment became a pain and a continual heartbreak before people who didn't even know them. They began to judge the child against their accelerated academic "E" achievements and citizenship awards. Yet even these measures could not demote the level of excellence in this child's life. They chronicled looking very intelligent, if not brilliant on record and reports, even excelling in spelling bees. Ultimately, even this level of excellence was enough to drown out what was said through obvious whispers. This person was an exceptional, honored student with high recommendations to skip grade levels but forced to tolerate the pains of criticism on a day-to-day school span. I fought back the tears picturing the disgust faced by this young individual, as if "the childhood blues" is not enough challenge prior to the years of preparation. Then later, it adds to this debt of an experience.

When I left this counseling session, I couldn't help to reimagine those moments they had experienced giving speech presentations, and the embarrassment and shame of high expectations being put on them in church or school platforms. Of course, they would stutter the entire time or become stuck on a word with their mouth open, eyes blinking, hands sweating, while shaking and standing still. OMG! I felt the agony in this individual's voice, just listening. They shared their perfect attendance in school throughout the horrific mid-west regional storms.

While other children were able to convince their parents or guardians to stay at home, this young individual didn't succeed in that matter. There was clearly a massive calling on their life to endure at a young age. I took a deep breath from counseling this young individual, as the conversation seem to become too much to continue. I said, "Let's take a break from this subject." They stood up and walked away. I immediately walked outside toward my vehicle. I began to release my own tears of sorrow. I had a reflective moment in my own childhood of a biblical scriptural passage I remembered reading; about a young man named Moses. In the book of Exodus, chapter 4, the arguments of intelligence between God and Moses began appearing.

Many of us wrestle with our inner struggles of preference to perform the tasks at hand. We tend to challenge the Creator in almost every way of how "our" abilities, gifts, and talents were to be used on the earth for a purpose that will stage to our Heavenly Father a presentation of glory as a response. Exodus chapter 4:10-17(MSG) reads:

> 10 Moses raised another objection to God: "Master, please, I don't talk well. I've never been good with words, neither before nor after you spoke to me. I stutter and stammer."
> 11-12 God said, "And who do you think made the human mouth? And who makes some mute, some deaf, some sighted, some blind? Isn't it I, God? So, get going. I'll be right there with you—with your mouth! I'll be right there to teach you what to say."
> 13 He said, "Oh, Master, please! Send somebody else!"
> 14-17 God got angry with Moses: "Don't you have a brother, Aaron the Levite? He's good with words, I know he is. He speaks very well. In fact, at this very moment, he's on his way to meet you. When he sees you, he's going to be glad. You'll speak to him and tell him what to say. I'll be right there with you as you speak and with him as he speaks, teaching you step by step. He will speak to the people for you. He'll act as your mouth, but you'll decide what comes out of it. Now take this staff in your hand; you'll use it to do the signs."

The message in this passage of scripture speaks. If we're honest, we all have a myriad of experiences of being rejected, overlooked, or treated as if we're not good enough.

As I reheard the heartache of this individual's testimony, this world has offered almost every human being a familiar life lesson to learn. The legendary, iconic actor and producer, James Earl Jones, had a similar story in his early career of rejection due to his speech impediment. He revealed the struggle in the discovery that this "speech problem" creates an inner jab at your self-esteem from the times you cannot respond. I remember reading an interview when he shared his inner struggle to communicate; how it really feels with the competition of articulating words in their simplest form to listeners, and they had no patience to hear him until the end. They could not wait until the competition ended and they took their seat in closing. James Earl Jones admitted, "that it was a painful moment." On a professional note, I remember attending a workshop, and someone quoting, "Public speaking is number one or two in rankings for fears to dying or grieving a death." It is very cumbersome to overcome anxiety in that time frame in front of anyone.

Side Thought- *Comedian, author, radio personality,* *Steve Harvey* *shared his testimony with his studio audience on his television show with a few people who were overcoming their stuttering issues. There, he admitted to a surprised following his terrible stuttering issue that he eventually overcame with conscious practice. Also, the awareness he gained on the importance of the consistency needed to maintain slower breathing and other techniques to continue a smooth flow in his speech. The public reality seems to be only susceptible to the "perfect looking and acting" people in order to accept them totally. Yet, whoever judges the audience to be the qualified examiners to qualify anyone? Let's talk about this later.*

Chapter Four

Picks and Chooses

Parenting has many variables when it comes to the guidance of our children at an early age. For the child, it is the most innocent time of learning from the parent/parents, peers, or family perspective. I call it the" bonding" days, lasting through the first year of development. So many eventful moments happen within this timeframe to many of us that have created a life of fortunes and misfortunes. Unfortunately, while some of the moments are beautiful, and cherished, others lead to heartbreak, confusion, dishonesty, carelessness, and selfishness. It is ideal to discover the presence of both responsible participants such as the parents in the upbringing of this beautiful gift called "child." Yet, the story begins for everyone uniquely different. We will probably never know the true household start, but we will learn years later what God's masterful intent for His creation was for us to be born.

Even though we're the product of our environment, we do have all the potential not to remain this way, since we were born into a greater "being."

Another passage in the Bible I read was authored by Matthew, stated in chapter 7:17-20, "...you will know them by their fruits." (NKJV). For the longest time while performing counseling sessions, mentoring, coaching, and discipleship, I understood the production of the family tree of behaviors to be wrong. Like many of us, I credited the parents' strong positions of sharing their theories and philosophies in upbringing their children with love, dignity, culture, and ethnic historical facts. I adore the outcomes and the pure hardworking individuals that made undeniable sacrifices under all circumstances for the sake of their children. My heart naturally goes out to all who made and are still making sacrifices to provide their best for their children. Yet, I failed by ignoring many of the silent philosophies and the pleasurable disciplines that were culturally encouraged to model for our children as a tool, to be an example for every generational heir that experienced more nonsense than common sense.

There are some toxic mindsets that were generated from damaged places from parental guidance for years and years prior that have crippled our children. Now adults, when these outcomes produce the next set of fruit, we often cannot begin to trace our silent questions of, "How did I get here? Why do I keep repeating this cycle?" And the answer is from "the them tree." So, when we read the text stating "know them," it's the tree that has these differences in "them" that teach lessons from wisdom, ignorance, or even brokenness. Therefore, when more children appear, they trigger an inner philosophical thought to impart to the innocent eyes of the little ones. Now the curiosities and wonders blossom to outcomes we may or may not like. If the child turns out as a fruitful, positive success, we began to accredit our egos and theories to ourselves, taking ownership of the rewarding gain. Yet, if the fruit is negative, we begin to blame it on the closest resembled image other than ourselves, so that we may shift the responsibility to the "probable cause" and not the tree. Too many times I have heard or learned of our parents tossing the blame of the child's outcome, be it positive or negative, placed on the parent that is absent, and that suits its validity. Likewise, in many cases, the present parent displays regular demonstrations before the child/children.

Then who can we blame? Say, "OUCH!" There's a time when God began to test parents' intuitiveness. He began to see if the parents have taken the credit of the children's greatness and excellence, and also, to identify if the child/children are destined for their life without their egos, successful credits over God's original plan and intent. Normally, this may showcase during the time the family is in a position for a family promotion. Yes, a family promotion. Meaning when at least one family member has invested their education, course/training completion, or some effort of achievement and it reflects on the support system, as we will immediately learn.

"Picks and Chooses" are done in the family among our elders and parents. The revered story of a dad named Jesse with his children surrounded by a king and men sent by God:

1 Now the Lord said to Samuel, "How long will you mourn for Saul, seeing I have rejected him from reigning over Israel? Fill your horn with oil, and go; I am sending you to Jesse the Bethlehemite. For I have provided Myself a king among his sons."

2 And Samuel said, "How can I go? If Saul hears it, he will kill me."
But the Lord said, "Take a heifer with you, and say, 'I have come to sacrifice to the Lord.'

3 Then invite Jesse to the sacrifice, and I will show you what you shall do; you shall anoint for Me the one I name to you."
4 So Samuel did what the Lord said, and went to Bethlehem. And the elders of the town trembled at his coming, and said, "Do you come peaceably?"

5 And he said, "Peaceably; I have come to sacrifice to the Lord. Sanctify yourselves, and come with me to the sacrifice." Then he consecrated Jesse and his sons, and invited them to the sacrifice.

6 So it was, when they came, that he looked at Eliab and said, "Surely the Lord's anointed is before Him!"

7 But the Lord said to Samuel, "Do not look at his appearance or at his physical stature, because I have refused him. For the Lord does not see as man sees; for man looks at the outward appearance, but the Lord looks at the heart."

8 So Jesse called Abinadab, and made him pass before Samuel.

9 Then Jesse made Shammah pass by. And he said, "Neither has the Lord chosen this one."

10 Thus Jesse made seven of his sons pass before Samuel. And Samuel said to Jesse, "The Lord has not chosen these."

11 And Samuel said to Jesse, "Are all the young men here?" Then he said, "There remains yet the youngest, and there he is, keeping the sheep."

And Samuel said to Jesse, "Send and bring him. For we will not sit down till he comes here."

12 So he sent and brought him in. Now he was ruddy, with bright eyes, and good-looking. And the Lord said, "Arise, anoint him; for this is the one!"

13 Then Samuel took the horn of oil and anointed him in the midst of his brothers; and the Spirit of the Lord came upon David from that day forward.

In my observation of young David, the eight children initiated the next century to everything in that family. The creator of humankind and the universe has this supernatural, unpredictable mindset above all mankind according to His plans on the earth. I believe for all children there's a divine plan purposed to explore great things regardless of your relatives, neighborhoods, community affiliations, and partner affairs. This is why WE MUST be careful with God's human property. There's a responsibility in managing what God accounts for us to manage rightly. Not perfect, but well to our best ability. David's beginning stages of purpose is obviously without his interest or permission to be king. In verse twelve of this passage, it highlights God's mindset publicly, including who and why David was born to become the next king openly. The text clearly refers to his father Jesse's initial preference of his brothers being selected as the next king, as if these were the only sons. In this moment of selecting one of his sons, I love God's overriding ability. He showed in front of man just how to promote the "overlooked" son, who carries the anointing and grace to perform God's strategic plan in the earth. Now, that's a powerful public signature.

In my thoughts, I recall many other clients sighing, "I have more than one brother or sister. There are several of us. What were my parents thinking?" Whew! OK! Too many families share this common epidemic of parents and peers, making differences among their children. Some secretly or outwardly ask and answer the questions, such as "Who's the smartest? Most giving? Most attractive? Most talented?" The list goes on and on. However, they don't realize how traumatic this debate can become to the preferred child over the qualified. This scenario is best explained in a counseling session from a client. It was a very sensitive topic due to their years of knowledge pertaining to their family tree. Yet I was expecting a different narrative. I hate to admit it, but I judged their personality, wardrobe, and the tone in their voice in this very moment. I had to apologize when it was over of my misjudgment, no different than what I read in the scripture verse seven, "...man looks at the outward appearance, but God looks at the heart." Mankind measures what qualifies to his standards, where God creates no limits.

The Monopoly Games Played

Oh, God, the games! Games, games, games. games, games, and more games. I know I have repeatedly written this word, but the "games" we've played speak nothing to maturity at the moment that we sometimes carelessly overlook the damage it creates in one's future, to the point of no return. The "Monopoly" board game created by Parkers Brothers, was first manufactured and sold in the year 1935 in the United States, and Waddington Publishing in the United Kingdom. They acquired the rights from Charles Darrow of Philadelphia, who developed the game in 1933. It continues to be produced as one of the oldest, unique, social board games for a family. Today, it continues the challenges with family's participating with countless, endless hours just to keep up. The silent foundation of this game is the mind-boggling strategies to win and reach rounds on the board between others. Here, you're competing against your opponents, while reaping the rewards of retaining power in property ownership and possession. Positive type of game style, right?

Well, unfortunately, for decades, we have applied these types of behaviors in our home life, and it has not always produced a positive outcome as we progress from our childhood to adulthood. If you pay close attention, you can see many similarities in our parents, uncles, aunts, seniors, and affiliate's behaviors from their background, plus years of their experiences being projected to others. Many have adopted several immoral, ungodly trends, yet appearing comfortably in relation to the "teachers" of their time. I believe we should accept the idea that people generally pick their teachers. Meaning, people have their favorite, preferred selects to listen to, as well as to receive from and to follow as recipients. Yes, I am certain even from our childhood, inner and outside influencers have provided a voice of impact to win our souls for reasons according to their beliefs, which can total a level of selfishness before one can identify their own self.

Deception is a real force to be reckoned with. To deceive anyone with various levels of influence forms a manipulative target to the innocent, including the vulnerable. This provides even more reason and insight to protect our children, elders, and naive ones with care and additional knowledge. Unfortunately, the power of the will can change by circumstance. Otherwise, it will cripple our developmental stages in learning that games never age, just the players. In the end, it hurts the unknowledgeable individuals with these tactics from a place of deception and evil. I once heard the word "evil" spells the word "live" backward. That word can be defined in different meanings based upon the route of one's lifestyle. Some may even argue that "perception is one's reality." The analytical parts of me cannot agree. It's a partial reality to this perception, because I may only have a perceiving view case upon case, but it's not "my" reality in character whatsoever. Again, we must be very careful of projecting our views to others to be taken as a universal truth.

Chapter Five

Not The Same As You May Think!

I decided to release my career to counsel those who are broken and risk-takers to move into a different business venture. Yet, God's plans for me have always shut me down every time. Subsequently, I felt the need to become transparent with the client individual I was serving at that moment. I can't even explain why all of a sudden, that taking a pause to reflect was necessary for my mental processing. Somehow, I suddenly felt I was becoming the patient of my own client to give a side of my history. I took a deep breath, exhaled the air, then I began to share. In the year 2000, I was awarded the most interesting opportunity to work for a community, one that has forever changed my life. Honestly, I was angry that the human resource department was so excited to offer me the opportunity, out of all of the applications I had applied to at that time. I absolutely hated this position. Again, I hated this position.

There was nothing exciting about the nature of work and the open position. It was my adult responsibility to supply income for my family and myself at that time. I remember reading the local job ad in several newspapers, stating, "If you have a heart for people with care and leadership, the Ray Graham Association for People with Disabilities welcomes you." I remember saying to myself, "What on earth compelled me to completely fill out this application without full thought of where it might lead?" Then, years later, it made perfect sense in various areas that really changed my life. On day one in the orientation, I was going through the excitement of being accepted for a position, after months of pursuing a particular career business that seemed incredible to launch. Now, I thank God for awarding me the opportunity.

I had the responsibility to provide care for residents in three apartments as a community support worker. I had the account-ability to care for gentlemen of the ages of twenty and thirty-five in one apartment, a sixty-year-old senior woman in another, as well as a couple with mental and physical disabili-ties. I had the duties ranging from changing diapers to being permitted to change sanitary napkins to the wife's monthly menstrual cycle. Imagine my discomfort in those moments. Oh, God! I cannot even begin to tell you how this era in my life begins to change my overall purpose in life. I became so confused as to how I got to a place called "here." My reality was that I felt I had failed in my direction, choices, and deci-sions. The only thing I could think of that made any sense to my pursuit to apply for this position, was me being desperate to have income to pay my bills on a consistent cycle. Just one year prior, I had received my professional Illinois State Barber styling license, and eventually, was able to work full-time as an entre-preneur salon owner. As a man, husband, father, and servant leader in my local community and a few faith-based opportuni-ties, I needed to provide, while also serving as one.

As time went on in my full-time position, I began to adapt and adjust to the full-time six a.m. schedule; to awake all the patients to begin their work/activity day. No one would believe me if I had to explain the running and fast pace on two or three different floors with stairs and elevators, I had to perform these tasks five days in a row. These patients depended on me with-out any excuses, or I would be the cause of them missing the most valuable activities needed in their physical, occupational, and speech developmental plans. The pressure of being reliable and exercising integrity in their homes was the weight of the entire experience.

All I could ask, quietly and randomly to myself was, "How did I begin to work with the handicapped and retarded people?" Sadly, I used to make sheer fun of them. In fact, many of my family and friends would make the noises, slob saliva, walk with limps, the whole complete seven descriptions, everything literally and figuratively wrong with them, and now I am working for them. Have you ever walked into a life-changing job that wasn't just a job, but a diverse chronicle view for your next phase in life? I've learned countless lessons regarding the divine change that is purposed by God. Unfortunately, many people are still baffled by one that puts on a "new man" and leaves the "old man" behind to become God's best. In the biblical book of Acts Chapter 9, Verses 10-17, there's a gentleman by the name of Paul. He was chronicled to leave from the city of Jerusalem to go to Syrian Damascus with a charge mandate issued by the high priest to seek out and arrest followers of Jesus, with the intention of returning them to Jerusalem as prisoners for questioning, then possible execution. God, however, interrupts this man's life with the ultimate purpose of creating a mark on earth ordained from Heaven. Let's take a look.

10 In Damascus there was a disciple named Ananias. The Lord called to him in a vision, "Ananias!"
"Yes, Lord," he answered.
11 The Lord told him, "Go to the house of Judas on Straight Street and ask for a man from Tarsus named Saul, for he is praying.
12 In a vision he has seen a man named Ananias come and place his hands on him to restore his sight."
13 "Lord," Ananias answered, "I have heard many reports about this man and all the harm he has done to your holy people in Jerusalem.
14 And he has come here with authority from the chief priests to arrest all who call on your name."
15 But the Lord said to Ananias, "Go! This man is my chosen instrument to proclaim my name to the Gentiles and their kings and to the people of Israel.

16 I will show him how much he must suffer for my name."
17 Then Ananias went to the house and entered it. Placing his hands on Saul, he said, "Brother Saul, the Lord—Jesus, who appeared to you on the road as you were coming here—has sent me so that you may see again and be filled with the Holy Spirit."
18 Immediately, something like scales fell from Saul's eyes, and he could see again. He got up and was baptized,
19 and after taking some food, he regained his strength.

Paul's conversion demonstrates God's lifetime purpose and power to divinely change a stubborn soul to a willing soldier. God was able to use his calling to righteousness by qualifying him while his past followers and witnesses did not prefer to receive from his "new" life conversion. Yes, Paul's history was used against him. He was not accepted but paid a great cost to endure the mandate of preaching the gospel.

*Side Thought-National Activist, American Christian Minister, **Dr. Martin Luther King Jr**. was a young, impactful spokesperson and leader for the civil rights movements, exhibiting passion and combatting truths against the odds of the laws on dangerous grounds and arenas. Dr. King continued to remain stern for the cause of injustices enforced to remain at the expense of lives being lost and ostracized. His historic speech, "I Have A Dream," left an impactful vision continually affecting lives beyond his own, even today.*

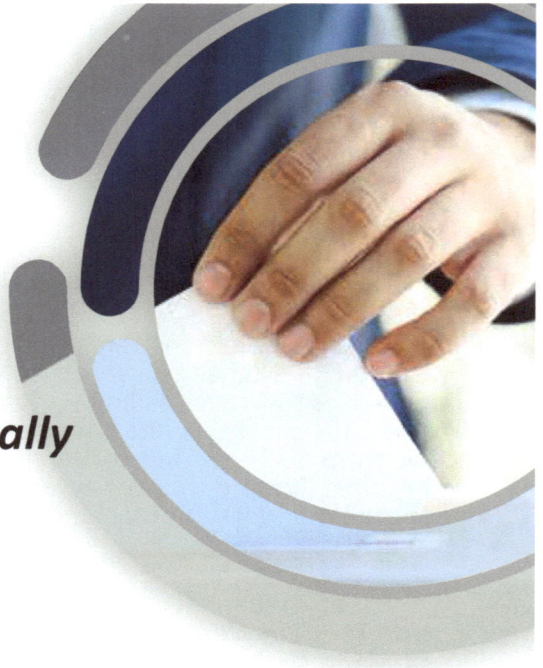

Chapter Six
Who Did You Really Vote For?

In taking these testimonial moments with the individual and myself, I came to a few conclusions I need to share. First, after twenty years in the professional public service industry, I am very closed-minded in areas. Many cannot admit this reality to be their own because of their image, but it is a truth that can make them free. More than before, I can accept that politics are everywhere, and in and affecting almost everything. This is one perspective; I believe it is a perception to many but in secret. Political treatment, decision making, as well as injustices, create wounds and warp opinions for a lifetime. Unfortunately, we regret this later, yet it excites us in the now. We create an elusive image of "how we think" it should represent our image with very temporal measures. From a generation of the old, I was thinking about the many employers that had given people a biased chance to become employees for their lucrative companies when they were children right through our adulthood. For many of us in this world, the employer makes a massive advertisement to the public but has no idea who may apply, walk-in, nor be recommended to become part of a team that will continue the mission statement; moreover, the philosophies of the company.

It is a very tender place of vulnerability to a great degree for that particular company on an on-going basis. Why? Because in the words of a film character, Forrest of Forrest Gump, he stated, "Life is like a box of chocolates; you never know what ya gonna get." Here are a few of our famous federal and state employer's disclaimer(s) that are expected to be exercised by employers for all applicants:

NONPROFIT does not and shall not discriminate on the basis of race, color, religion (creed), gender, gender expression, age, national origin (ancestry), disability, marital status, sexual orientation, or military status, in any of its activities or operations. These activities include, but are not limited to, hiring and firing of staff, selection of volunteers and vendors, and provision of services. We are committed to providing an inclusive and welcoming environment for all members of our staff, clients, volunteers, subcontractors, vendors, and clients.

Or

Equal Opportunity Employer - All qualified applicants will receive consideration for employment without regard to race, color, religion, sex, sexual orientation, gender identity, gender expression, national origin, age, protected veteran or disabled status, or genetic information."Both clauses are mandates for employers to exercise when hiring and training individuals. It has been a law criterion that has been issued to institutes in the training of all recruiters and human resource developers across the nation when interviewing new applicants.

By mentioning both disclaimers, whether s modeled in the non-profit or for-profit communities (public services or faith-based/ministry organizations), many have failed to properly staff and train leaders in leadership under these laws. The deception of politics in these arenas has caused more confusion than good at times, by trusted leaders requiring the responsibility of placing the personalities to grow. Eligibility is weighed high in these groups because of the brand representation. There's no such thing as a perfect profile team; just effective production is where the focus should be.

Teenage Checkers

With this in mind, imagine the pre-screening process conducted by the hiring staff for a teenager with no background, resume, experience, or possibly not a referral to decide the functions and operations for their team. I prefer this natural approach as a preference beyond the qualification criteria. These are some of the purest moments when an individual can have an opportunity after an observation based on their heart, persistence, attitude, eagerness, goals to learn and grow in character value. As I think about it, I remember one of my children having their first job interview as a teen at McDonald's in 2012; I almost cried. As much as I knew about her qualities, strengths, and weaknesses, I was so nervous for them. I guess you will say, "Why?" Well, the older you become, the more you will experience the unfair judgments in leadership and management in our human resource departments. These judgments come from those that will become supercritical in their selection of recruiting members to form an excellent team. Think about it. Just how discouraging does it become, applying to an intimidating establishment for employment, and you're already rejected before you can submit your application entry? Or, in some cases, you read the qualifications and requirements, then you ask yourself, "Can I really perform in this position when hired? Will they even call me for an interview?" Or how about acknowledging, if you have a physical or mental health condition, how this will hinder you from being considered a candidate for this position?

Such defeatism is bound to conquer the psyche and emotions from the fear of rejection. We have faced this type of defeat, whether we like to admit it or not. The checker game of deciding a side to play against your opponent, taking jumps with a strategy to dominate your opponent, whether you have verbal experiences from others to participate in this game. As a teen, you may potentially recognize and instill a valuable lesson before your adulthood that many people, regardless of age, race, gender, religious, and social affiliations have a game to apply to their life for their next chapter in their journey. Luckily, for those that believe in luck or what I call the "by chance" perspective, know that the back of the red and black checkerboard is the ultimate goal to success. The furthest back row of the game board is staged to achieve the king's position of authority with strategy and techniques. In my personal thoughts, the good ole winning style of my dad taught me as a teenager the maneuvering tools regarding life and politics. In fact, I can recall his excitement, and the names of the older gentlemen teaching this particular game that helped him apply street wisdom in addition to his wit toward everything that requires strategy.

My dad's philosophy would trend to "Get the lessons now, and when you get older, you can handle anything." Notice the television episodes and films featuring the teens and "checker games" of vision, jumping to an adult challenge of living, then sustaining and later, the peer pressure to be "somebody." More now than before, we've listened to the individual's background of reflection, brought by continuous inner sights. I have forced myself to muffle. In numerous psychology courses, we'd learned the philosophy and perspectives of the tender adolescent years in child development up until adulthood. Yet the tender teenage years are the grooming preparatory time period that can create your head start outlook on life, or it can possibly deviate the teen's sensitive attention to another route to pursue. More importantly, we're never in control when we are born. However, the way our delivery brings us here will transform the world into pieces.

*Side Thought- Renowned author and lecturer, **Hellen Keller,** was born healthy until 19 months later when she became deaf and blind. Growing from infancy into childhood, she mentally and emotionally fought a growth functionality label as wild and unruly. Helen Keller became a braille reader, installed as a standard system for the blind around the world. She influenced the attention of the U.S. government to make the blind population noticeable and also to change the lives of many that traveled the world, producing hope, courage, and humility with limited resources, if any.*

Chapter Seven

You're Not As Weird
As "they" Think

The individual and I returned back into my office, days after taking all we had learned. We allowed all of the realizations of not being preferred to educate our curiosity, personally, and as a people. First of all, we should break the barrier thoughts of how God our creator, designed us as a gift to the world. Unique is the descriptive word I would like to use to describe our personality and character. Some people claim "weird" is not a negative definition. Quite often, the word "strange" is probably the better description to anyone or anything that is not easy to figure out. I came to understand the more people you'll meet, the more you will learn about yourself. This can include your biases, prejudices, racism, and indifferences; they will tell on your inner character every time you are in environments that cause one to accept the other's originality. Originality is what will make everyone special in the eyes of God and man. As a counselor and a lover of God's people, I had to grow into this position of maturity. No one will ever be you! I repeat, no one will ever intend to think, taste, smell, dream, love, earn, serve, eat, feel, learn, walk, breathe, obtain habits, overcome, undercome, triumph, conqueror, work, strategize, support, neglect, reject, vacation, object, or anything as a living human being. We also must look high in the sky and speak outwardly that we have no control over our introduction. I remember writing a poem called "No Control of This" found in my book **Speechless Conversation**, as it reads:

No Control Of This

My physical features, My gender, My birth parents,My intellect, My abilities, My disabilities, My birthplace, My background, My skin complexion, My family, My honest initial attractions, Other People's jealousy, Envies, Gossip, Rumors, The weather, Court decisions, Allergic Reactions, People motives, The color of nature, No say so, Who loves me, who likes me, who tolerates me, and maybe celebrates me, My relationship with who, The leadership we inherited,
And territory we all have, Why continue to endure the pressure of figuration when I only have the power over what was given to me? My hands are tied for this very reason; understanding my blessed hands don't even belong to me.

Chapter Eight

But, I Don't Look Like Them

Yes, you heard me. I don't look like "them." "Heck, not only do I not look like them, I don't act like them, nor sound like them," is what I've said in numerous settings. In these particular settings, it has made me feel what I call "exclusion of importance." What do I mean? I mean the "not included" feeling is not just a feeling, but a reality when one experiences similar reactions and treatments of rejections or non-invitations caused by the biases of not looking the part or qualified to "our" standards of inclusion. This is another thin line of courtesy, one that silently expects similar results when these moments occur. If you really think about it, we may not get to all of the unqualified scenarios we may see here in our lifetime. But when it's all over, we're incredibly qualified to do more than what we credit ourselves to become responsible for achieving. For some reason, the failures of things have become a marker to our greatness, and that's an opportune truth to accept. Failure, denials, or delays do not disqualify our eligibility in any form whatsoever.

Handicapped, Disabled, Mentally Ill

These three impairments hold a great, special, tender place in my heart along the journey of my career and family. As I mentioned in chapter five, I once served as a community support worker for a disability and handicapped organization. Now, years after the additional education, I advanced as a clinical case manager in this vast public service industry. This is the field of study that has greatly changed my life as it pertains to the compassion and support of beautiful people. At one point in my life, I was not recognizable to serve as a leader, because I was a disguised, second-hand instigator. I enjoyed the immature jokes and critical views of others around me. It was very cruel to mimic their innocence at that time. It brings me to tears as I recollect my behavior as if I was perfect or above their deformity. Besides myself, many readers may know of someone that carries this similar attitude. The attitude of thinking you're a "better" person and your "better" self qualifies you above others. The uneducated are commonly masking their ignorance in this delicate area. The mystery of it all is that life can turn the corner for us, and it has no prejudices to whom it may affect. The illusion that we will always continue with good looks, wealth, and a popular, positive attitude can become a misconception for the self-righteous, unteachable subjects. Unfavorably so, there is a group of people that are very mean-spirited to the selects, with arrogance and a pompous posture. Imagine mixing this group inside of a set culture to cooperate in harmony. It will take some humility and openness in character like you would not believe.

These are common indicators to remind the human race that we're not in competition with our side components nor neighbors, but with our primary, original purpose, we were designed to perform. It can be very elusive to assume that every single individual has the exact same reason to be born on this planet. Let's observe this thought in perspective. For every incredible person that was "fearfully and wonderfully made" (Psalms 139:14; NIV), God, the Creator was not designated to produce and perform on this earth for the same reasons to bring

Himself glory. In fact, it is a measure of one's willingness to discover and manage it well as good stewards. "If you are faithful over a few things, I will make you ruler over many." (Matthew 25:23; NIV)

Chapter Nine

You're More Than Enough

I can't imagine being alone in my thought process when it comes to the experiences of what I call "measuring up" or being enough for people. I believe you can attest to this chapter in multiple ways. I will risk saying that every human cringes at the hint of this feeling. Many would say in their defense, "I know who I am or what I bring to the table." But what we hate to admit is how we all need people to help us progress.

Without the participation of others helping and assisting us, we wouldn't be who or where we are. WE NEED PEOPLE! Yes, I shall scream it again. WE NEED PEOPLE! What is interesting to wonder is...what qualified our ancestry to set the standards for others? How do "they" know that what was given to them as a quality sets the bar for excellence and exceptionality. For example, who educated those to write our constitutional laws and ordinances in our countries? Who graded the papers of those children with limited information and resources? Or who permitted those decades upon decades that were allowed to install laws that are still in place today? Hmm...have you ever wondered? What we can potentially agree upon is many of the laws, inventions, and creative trends were God's plan.

His purpose was implemented in all of His children that were never perfect. Take a minute to process that thought to the best of your imagination. Experiment with your intellect and senses until some type of venture, idea, or invention forms with your participation in the process and outcome.

After all of this, to think about the families, tribes, organizations, companies, and group affiliates, sometimes we can yet feel the need to ask, "Am I enough?"

No, you're not enough in the eyes of men and women who require validation as well vindication to convince themselves of who you are. I read a quote once that affirms, "Never waste your time trying to explain who you are to people who are committed to misunder-standing you." I know, I know...it is unbelievable that someone in the human flesh can commit to this type of behavior. These are just a few character types of people you may want to reevaluate your affiliations with. If you're not careful, you may become ensnared, then can be subtly enticed to lose your identity while second, third, or fourth guessing yourself. The Quora.com presents on the world-wide website a few characteristics of the types we encounter in many diverse settings:

Unsympathetic - uncaring, they can't seem to put themselves into a situation of the person, country, etc., and feel the personal agony that would go with such an experience

Controlling - often demean or criticize others as a means of building themselves up and appearing superior and in control

Opinionated - hold strong opinions, think their opinion matters much more than yours, which is not always true, of course.

Domineering - engage in aggressive and controlling behavior to secure and stabilize their surroundings.

Narcissistic - excessive need for admiration, disregard for other's feelings, a sense of entitlement

Double-standard - unfair treatment. Principles apply differently and usually more rigorously to one group of people or circumstances than that to another.

These are common character personalities found through relationships I have discovered in counsel. They will also impact an experience that will impactfully alter your innermost questions during your series of self-evolution and discovery to become your best self. These evaluations are very important to examine if you're not discerning carefully or placing them in a group to entertain.

The "Side Dude or Side Chick"

This saying or term "the side chick or the side dude" became a popular, now common term used in reference to an extended, outside relationship. This assumption by the persuasion of the other party that has placed you in their lives with secondary or no value as a high priority of valuable treatment. Ladies and gentlemen, I must admit that this subject matter is not the most comfortable to expound upon because many have been made to feel as a benefit, not as a qualitative, exceptional candidate for whatever the relationship deems great. So many times, we missed the true terms of the relationship we entered or were persuaded to entertain. Very unfortunate in most cases, yet in older relationships, you'll be surprised at the level of superficial foundations that they were based upon. In friendships, we qualify and disqualify them all of the time, based upon what they do or what they can do. I learned in college the "W.I.I.F.M. Effect" (meaning "What's in It for Me") is one of the obvious, silent motives in most relationships labeled as friendships. I never knew it was a label for this type of concept. Although it's been used in business sales for quite some time with a prospect or potential customer, I find it commonly relevant and sound in most unconventional dealings and settings.

Pimps, prostitutes, rotating relational flings, friends with benefits, or even escorts are not much different than some tenured relationships and marriages, mistreating their mate negatively with fantasies of past affairs in the forefront. Whether it begins inwardly and manifests outwardly, it is not acceptable to exercise. In some cases, you're the "side" or manifesting that title in the end. You're no longer a prefer-ence, but a liability. Eventually, you'll become disrespected, and without honor because of the supply you once rendered. Now, you no longer can provide to their satisfaction. It is a useless disposition to experience. This level of discomfort you will experience is unforgettable. To be thrown away after this utilization is known to devastate the purest intents of one's soul.

> **Side Thought**- Classic film, "I AM Sam" featuring, **Sean Penn**, acting as the mentally Ill single man challenged to raise a newborn child that was left and discarded by the natural mother without notice. The municipal courts felt the father was not qualified nor preferred to continue parenting the toddler, due to his mishap of abandonment and his mental and physical disability. Yet, we may award a handicapped senior citizen guardianship for a minor due to negligent irresponsibility of the natural parent's absence.

Chapter Ten

I Can Live With It

After a period of differential treatment from naturally dysfunc-
tional humans comes the point of acceptance you must rest in,
and that is to say, "I can live with it." Yes, you can. In fact,
you're already living with these realities. I never knew I would
be able to until I agreed to own my testimonies, then I gently
wrote them out as a testament. Although it is not and never
will be an easy thing to do, but "easy" and "tough" do not mix.
There's a part of us that will often invite the "easy" (not as
much effort) in almost anything that demands effort, yet the
tough approach comes with numerous amounts of prices one
eventually pays. I can hear that you may ask, "What kinda cost
do you mean, sir?" In specific moments of being ignored or
overlooked, the discomfort creates a cyclone of emotions and
obfuscate decisions that are unhealthy in the unpreferred or
unselected. I can see an individual sitting in the back of a
room at a particular event, watching the activity in front of the
room with all of the "needed" attention that is expected. The
common expectations from respondents with the exuberant
phenomenon excluded the less emotional, unelected, unen-
thusiastic section that was simply overlooked as if they

would like to receive the same treatment with an option to participate. This scenario does not necessarily mean that the peculiar ones are incapable or have anywhere to go. There's just a calm matter in which all should be categorized to qualify the "majority rules." This is a bullying attitude.

The "Under Dog"

This is one of the most elicit, positional titles of treatment to the overlooked and underestimated individual. The "underdog," the team or person that looks unequipped, has no prestige, nothing to be proud of, and, in most cases, no consideration to succeed or to have top-notch ability according to the views of man. The appearance in various ways was embarrassing, in the most honest confession I've had to convey. In some cases, it may not be as attractive to the cosmos in general. The measurements are slim to none when receiving appealing preferences from others. According to our international world wide web, the term "underdog" is a competitor thought to have little chance of winning a fight or contest in anything. The underdog character creates an instant doubt in some minds of not having any possibility, potential, or dominance, BUT the component is credited in whatever the original mutual race is determined by. For some, "the underdog" is not the most attractive person or team to join. Your chances of becoming one of the noticeable perks of catering from the public and private eyes are slim to none. Some would say the "underdog" is the "by chance" or the "fixed" opponent in comparison.

But for a lot of others, the "underdog" is the unexpected sneak from the back door, underestimated, powerful, labeled, an inconspicuous candidate with huge courage presented, sometimes quietly. I heard in conversations sometimes as a people we can "fall asleep" as in not be aware of the non-popular. There are times the "underdog" simply means the "non-mainstream" person. There's no need to make an announcement for this type of group because the surprising results will produce credibility one way or another.

Though the underdog may not always gain the favorable choice of winning, inasmuch, the odds stacked against the preferred one shows the courage as well as the conquering attitude shockingly to any audience. The individual reveals further examples. There have been plenty of times in their physical education class the individual with their classmates would be examining the "popular" picking teams to play any sports pertaining to the class. They would predictably choose the notably healthy, loudest, familiar ones to save the fame and fun for the moment. Never mind that the few times the instructor's instructions were to pick other classmates different from before, and now the sighs and mockery openly captures the energy of the room.

Chapter Eleven

"No Credit Again"

From the individual's written portfolio of their childhood years, they remembered attending mandatory church. They were expected to stay long hours and attend weekly with their grandparents, aunts, uncles, and cousins. Enough hours to stay all morning, noon, and evening. They would enjoy all the moments of attending church, as long as any of their favorite cousins were coming to endure the long hours alongside them. They continue to write their experiences, like seeing their grandmother along with other great women volunteering their service for cooking meals in the kitchen to accommodate the leaders and congregants throughout the long days. The mothers would form a lunch menu to cook and prepare nights before to present and add to the menu. The leaders in this ministerial group would be in charge of all the young children and teens, including young adults, to assist in making the meals a success before the end of the worship service. They remember seeing themselves being recruited by the hard-working mothers in the hot kitchen just in time. Then came the announcements over the loud microphone for the week, which also included today's menu to tempt the congregation's appetites.

That is also when the aromas appeared from all the great cooking in the church since the early morning arrivals of the discipleship. Now, when it comes to the end of worship, the leaders are to pilot the lunch meals first. The prayer of grace is spoken outwardly before the meals are distributed. At this moment, they can remember hearing the compliments of the meals given to the department chairperson only. They waited several times, just as before, and would only notice one name was recognized for the strong effort of making these delicious meals possible. As if this food preparation and presentation was completely created and accomplished by one person! They have often seen the hunger for recognition from team members striving for excellence under the pretense given to the leaders with honor, just to be overlooked and not recognized in front of their circle. By all means, if there's any sacrifice of food pantry items taken from the unnoticeable, unrecognized team members, this would ultimately disappoint the meaningful purpose of joining. The "no credit left behind" combination will explain the weekly sad faces. The reactions of feeling unappreciated don't complement the efforts of these loving people or the volunteering of their time of service. Over and over, we treat such people to serve others with our entire heart's intent but never seeing the recognition or appreciation. Qualified to create the end goal but not preferred to recognize, gain credit nor support for the work effort it requires to accomplish these results of success. So many of us have experienced this type of cost to our character:

- Healthy Self-Esteem to Low Self-Esteem.

- Self-Worth to Loss of value.

- Full Excitement to No Motivation.

- Low Momentum to Zero Drive Achievement.

- Optimistic Overachiever to Pessimistic Underachiever.

- Sharp and Glamorous to an Overlooked Wholistic Man or Woman.

- Loving and Great Spirited to the Mistreatment of others.

- Trustworthiness to Over-guarded.

Side Thought - *Inventor and businessman **Thomas Alva Edison** was described as America's greatest inventor. Many devices, such as sound recording, motion pictures, mass, and communication, were developed by him, according to Wikipedia. He was a special-needs, very hyperactive and difficult child prone to distractions, with loss of hearing in both ears due to sickness and a physical injury from a conductor. He invented 1,093 patents; the phonograph, the incandescent light bulb, and motion picture camera were the most popular inventions. Incredible testimony for a kid to have a disability and to be homeschooled by his parents at that time.*

Another Side Thought - *Although Thomas Edison was nationally recognized as the inventor of the light bulb, African American **Lewis Howard Latimer** played a major part in the invention of the light bulb development with Edison. In 1881, Latimer patented a style of carbon filaments to allow the bulbs to burn for long durations at a time. Thomas Edison is credited for the invention of the lightbulb, while the innovation of a long-lasting carbon filament was created by Latimer.*

Chapter Twelve

The Disqualification Effect

There's an obvious underlying thought of reality that comes to my mind as an adult when the childhood elementary teachings of "cause and effect" takes place. The drillings of this teaching had no importance to me at that particular stage of my life, but Oh... it most certainly fits my comprehension of all of the life lessons I have observed and learned since. To every cause, there's an effect theory that has a guaranteed impact on every encounter accompanied by a warranty. In other words, there's no way around it. With every cause, an effect is going to happen. As a people, we seem to lose sight of the effects we risk, whether it is an intentional or unintentional cause rendered. This is especially true of those that cause a lifetime of damage and time that is beyond repair for many cases. I often teach the differences between the character flaws of performing actions of "dumb," "ignorant," or "stupid."

There are so many variances of repercussions from the effects. For example, if any male or female has been molested or raped, the chance of a committed relationship later in life is commonly not promised, but an infidelity relationship may be at risk due to the innocent cause of this effect. Here's another example: when you break the trust of an open heart that dared to risk an exclusive relationship after years of protective, judgmental, and overly critical treatment. They then decide to bask in a relationship with you. You've not only violated their trust and personal space but confirmed to them that their fears, when you've taken the same type of risk, would further a very familiar damaged agenda like before. Now, the disqualifications for one's future take activation. The violation of respect tears deep. It leaves new scars on old wounds, damaging the soul to this effect. Therefore, as a human, any tampering with the soul creates an entire lifestyle for one.

For example, The Soul (Psyche)consists of the mindset, willingness and emotions.

"Will" Alignment

The soul part of mankind is an undeniable workshop inside of every living human being. Since the creation of man, the soul is what separates the human living organisms from plants and animals. The study of mankind consists of three parts, such as the spirit (pneuma), body (soma), and soul (psyche). Particularly, the soul encompasses the mindset, emotion, and willingness to the section of our body temple that will always be a constructive project. How am I able to make such a statement? Well, without the willingness of having a thermostat to gauge its level of power to permit change or permanence, it will continue to exist, but will not progress. Progression is a personality by itself. Progression is a verb in acting above a noun. Therefore, the willingness for one to accept any state of the condition while the opponent has the will to give credence is a consistent realignment in itself. This alignment can always become the remedy for all that matters the most, and that is love. Love is the only person, yes, person, redeemed by modelized and standing high to barricade against the odds.

The "disqualified" in the eyes of man has depleted options to receive God's masterpiece of humankind, as one of the extreme exhibits God has ever bragged upon to say "it was good" after the creation was completed from this point of view, according to the book of Genesis 1:31. The power in oneself will determine any manner of dynamic strength and manifestation from within. But how would anyone ever know of these two dynamics, unless the alignment of one can merge with a purpose to carry out the needed actions?   For years of my community observation, I would hear the frustration of many that would blame unproductivity to leaders only, versus the team unit following the team's leadership. You may have the leadership with the charge, but the dissolution from the unwilling individuals disturbs the excitement to create and fulfill a vision. Emotions are the result of mindset productions and the will's permission to activate it all.

Chapter Thirteen

Preferences and Qualifications

In the end, God makes preferences and qualifies the called according to a biblical text in 1 Corinthians 27:29. Throughout this book, you may have identified with or can relate to similar examples of something that reminds you of an injustice, a time of care that was improperly handled with the best pure intention. I would even risk to state you were probably one that was victimized in a similar type of position, but without being aware, the initiator performing the injustice and prejudice acts as politically instructed or out of insensitive immaturity. Whatever state you found yourself in during the chapter case studies, it may benefit you to level your humility and carefully examine yourself regarding such behavior. There is God-given grace (recipient of what one does not deserve) and mercy (not receiving what one deserves) that God grants to his children who may acknowledge what was given to all mankind as a gift, not an entitlement.

There's a security with God to those He justifies and set apart for and with Him. Those are the ones he prefers, meaning you. You may read this entire book. You will argue with your surroundings, circumstances, background, family, weaknesses,

as well as mistakes, yet God made no mistake on His appoint-ment with your life. Your life was marked before you came into the knowledge of learning all and everything you are. Every-thing that has happened to you does not disqualify you from greatness and a blessing you were destined for according to God's standards. There's a host of people in your life that may see it differently, but that is only an unforeseen opinion that is premature to the potential of greatness you may have yet to experience. I wouldn't give up based upon your progress report you've already given yourself. It is not fair to yourself to cancel your destiny appointments just because it's difficult to recognize all that you are preferred and qualified to achieve. Activate the provinces that were disqualified by your delusion-al opponents, even if you enacted yourself as a contradictive enemy. Meditate on 1 Corinthians 1:27-29 (NIV) in the bible as a reference. You will notice it reads, verse:
27 But God chose the foolish of the world to shame the wise; God chose the weak things of the world to shame the strong.
28 God chose the lowly things of this world that are not to nullify the things that are.
29 So that no one may boast before him.

If you decide not to read the biblical text, there's evidence all around that breeds hope, potential, and resilience that is formulated inside every human being. These aspirations can do more than you can even ask or think according to that power that works within you. Qualified and Preferred individu-als take a different initiative to adjust their outlook on the obvious, with a mature posture from before and decide their outcome from a mature place of healing and exhortation.

Side Thought- *The song, "I Can't Make You Love Me" by* **Bonnie Raitt**, *rings a bell to my heart and many across the world. In my observation, it doesn't matter how great your profile appears on paper, what "you may bring to the table," money or pedigree obtained in your qualifications, you can't make anyone love, see, and respect the value you possess.*

THE REVELATION

Throughout these case studies of scenarios, I realized how tremendously I have grown by simply listening and processing this transparent, life-changing individual. The more the individual shared, the less I cared to cover their triumphs and victories won throughout all the years of mishaps and misfortunes. One would say, "I completely put myself out there," and yes, I did. I eventually gained the courage and asked this individual if I could utilize their authentic life experiences with others that may read a few pages of this book as an encouraging healing aide to holistic health (mind, body, and soul). By doing so, it will become a conscious declaration to ALL of your life's dangers, misunderstandings, and misfortunes that God permitted on this journey, as he enlisted the masses of the chosen people that He Qualifies and He Prefers as His priority before you were born.

Ladies and gentlemen, please help me welcome to your open hearts, family, friends, circle of influences, and some of the most lucrative, busiest, relevant people you may know, your coworkers, leaders, and every young lad and gal... My Story. Yes, I am "the individual," and this is My Story! Reader, you may be shocked to your very core or baffled in your conscience, but this confession cost me something. I teach periodically, "When you are free, you can share anything to help someone." That is the aspiration of this book. I am determined to share my love with you. There's nowhere in the world to be found a "perfect man" for your acceptance in this book because there's no one in the world that ever exists. Excitedly, I have a perfect narrative I lived to overcome, but I did not ask to carry it out. I would like to apply a popular quote by Maya Angelou that simply says, 'When someone shows you who they are, believe them the first time."

That's the blessing God wanted you to see about you and I. You see, I may not have had your exact narrative in the lines and pages of this book as I interviewed this "individual," and I looked through the mirrors of my life paths. I then wrote down the bad, the ugly, the terrible, the low esteemed, the undeserving, the double-minded, the overthinker, the minority, the stutterer, and how much more God keeps for himself to share as needed. Your inner person that may secretly carry shame, guilt, or your masked image that you dare to share hears your innermost cry. I was born to help you and you will live again. As of NOW! Sometimes we can read and hear stories that can very well hit your home base for holistic healing. Many will quickly reject the necessary healing for your efficient soul, but I encourage you to direct this information to a fellow. Please, do not forfeit this time. I repeat. Do not forfeit this time. I understand you may not want to cry anymore because of the damage of feeling underestimated, used, abandoned, not enough, excuses, lies within lies, and much more. Yet, you will not end in the way(s) your experience has taken you. You're better for it all. I am confident in this belief!

Another Candid Confession

Not only have I been victimized by all the scenarios, and many more, I have been guilty of doing some of the same to others. I have preferred others in dating relationships over a few who gave all the things I deemed as qualifications to be my life partner. I have misjudged and employed the "better looking" or "most skillful" (on paper or referred as) and I overlooked the non-experienced, dedicated candidate loyal with integrity. I have been political (by my leadership) to exercise such behavior in various settings that would've cost my career, but for the sake of looking "qualified and preferred," I felt I would lose my relevance to the "onlookers" to avoid the "naysayers."

Not keeping in mind those groups of people who are all assembled as one to make you confident that you were ALREADY built and preferred by God and your calling is qualified by your creator, not people's opinions.

The Realization...

*I can relate...*to those individuals who have been playing for your wage increase at your workplace and were NEVER considered or recognized for your hard work. You have been faithful, prompt, and persevered through the critical judgments from your fellows, yet the most talked about.

*I can relate...*to being told by countless employers that your skillset doesn't amount enough for reputable compensation to avoid applying for more jobs just to maintain your responsibilities.

*I can relate...*to working in bands and groups for several years, and never being told you were officially "a part" of the group while jokes and sarcasm were being said when you entered the room, during work shifts, and after you made an exit. Also, you witnessed employers interviewing others in your presence that was talented with charisma and exciting propaganda given to the crowd but exhibited poor attendance as well as unprofessional morals during your faithful, professional, consistent, and exceptionally performed tasks due to the calling of God.

*I can relate...*to taking the frustrations of the political games and turning them all into goals to become a mastery of accepting "no" as your answer to enter. Then completing higher education, taking courses, and increasing your skill sets just to be rejected AGAIN to now being "overqualified" or a threat in the midst of your peers. Go figure!

*I can relate...*to desiring a healthy, blessed, harmonious, loving relationship with plans to build trust, fidelity, and an exclusive, unpenetrated partnership to later learn your mate that they desired to prefer careers, extended families traditions, former soul-tie covenants, children, and hang-ups to overrule your original covenant agreement. They secretly changed their minds, being free-willed.

*I can relate... .*to witnessing parents making betrayal covenants with your siblings as their favorites while living vicariously through your hard work and strengths and courageous life, while intimidated to invest in the chosen expert God called you from birth that is ordained to set captive minds free.

*I can relate...*to having to exercise professionalism, love, integrity, generosity, and patience (*just to name a few*) to those who are heavily, emotionally, and mentally bruised. They are marked by years of repeated scars, mental and physical molestation, confusion, and lack of respect, yet still exhibit true love, grace, and mercy towards others as well as themselves.

There's no such thing as a perfect human being. So, let's dispel the "I'm Not Perfect" disclaimer as the license issued for asking grace and mercy to be an exception with no rules. We are fearfully and wonderfully made by God as humans to perform the unimaginable power. We retain an authoritative posture; no one else is customized to display it the way we're warranted.

I Noticed....I AM Not the Only One

I am not the only one. I am not the only individual found stereotyped by various political systems and broken constituents placed on a path to gain courage. Nor am I the only one with a fevered tenacity to recognize obvious wickedness, and discerning the unethical infrastructures that were designed for selfish gain and to overpower the souls of mankind.

Forgiveness, Love and Courage

Forgiveness, love, and courage are three of the most powerful people you can ever meet to soar as a preferred qualified individual. I have identified these three words as people. They are nouns and verbs, to be quite frank. As nouns (person, place, or thing), your character will speak for it all. Traits of true forgiveness, love, and exhibiting courage will communicate moral, ethical, and spiritual character benefiting the receptor, as demonstrated by the initiator. As a verb, you must become this person.

Forgiving, love and courage and apply action to forgiving, loving, and being courageous to overcome this human epidemic. Every human was purposely created by God to be original; fortunately, it is going to cost everyone in their lifetime. You must "Be Forgiving, Be Love, Be Courage." Be this person as you come into the purpose you were born to be. This is the only way your true character will exhibit exceptional qualities and escape the criteria of "me" and formulate your discovery in your journey. You will no longer be in the bondage of people's criteria, just to be found eligible for their approvals. Liberality means nothing but a falsity of hope to the imprisoned inmate who may never experience this dimension of freedom. For the cost is too much to be yourself, different, uniquely original and a threat to the ignorance of an enclosed mind. That is quite a price tag to throw away. No matter how much you try to mimic your mentors, leaders, and superiors, you should only want to apply needed inspiration and wise principles to continue being the forgiving, courageous, and loving person you were created for in this life. This is a value money or currency can NEVER purchase or be negotiated by.

It's Gonna Cost You to Be Yourself

As I stated before in these chapters, from your parents, superiors, and peers throughout your lifetime the majority wants to "take credit" for who you are, what you are, your education or skill set training, what you've accomplished, or even the looks of your potential before their eyes. All of them want you to model them, take from this class, apply their methodology, don't change the "will." Therefore, it takes courage to bypass the voices of those in your passing in order to venture into your "true Identity" on the earth. There's something very significant about God's creation of you to place you on the earth as a testament of faith and relevance that to God's plans, not the plans people have had for us all along.

Yes, it will continue to cost you a lifetime of losing and releasing, learning and unlearning, defeating the odds and evens, withstanding and withdrawing, and to love things, places, and ideas as you continue in all assignments.

These perspectives will definitely qualify your will to be with yourself, for others, by yourself, and watch yourself grow stronger and do not take offenses personally anymore. Offenses are everywhere all around us every day. It takes much effort to reach your hand out to take offense versus taking offenses and making it personal.

I read this bible scripture that reads, "For whoever wants to save their life will lose it, but whoever loses their life for me will find it." Matthew 16:25 (NIV). This is interpreted to decide to lose yourself (identity, culture, and status) in your lifetime and insert your soul into your God creator and permit His leadership and knowledge regarding your sole purpose to simply come alive in the original purposes planned for your life. You will discover only God qualifies, calls, equips and leads you into all truths about you, absent from the stereotypes, labels, names, class types, and categories from outside of your skin.

You Can Be Yourself. Just BE! Stop the bleeding to prove that you need to become. Naturally and supernaturally, that BE will transpire. Free yourself and just simply Be to become what your calling mandates you to be.

ACKNOWLEDGEMENTS

To my amazing parents: Mrs. J. Louise Sims and the late Woodroe "Popps" Sims. YOU ARE MY WORLD! I pray that you remain proud of every publication and adventure I am able to conquer. You're always my rock and tear droppers at the mention of strength, fidelity, and teamwork.

To my incredible siblings: Shemeka, Natasha, Kenya, Kyla, Shawn, Kimberly, and Tawanda, you are my forever international support system of love...whether I hear from ya or not I Love You! LOL SMH!

To my accountable siblings: Emma, Woodie, Jamecia, and Jaiz - you ALWAYS keep this eldest brother proud and in-line with a prayer life to heaven. Near or far, you guys keep the noise joyful. I Love You!

To my life-educator, MY "BabyLady" Ebony L. Sims. Daughter, you're ALWAYS here, there, and everywhere with me at the same time. Daddy loves you!

To my beautiful grandmother, Missionary Lorine Holman, I always have you in mind when every door opens at the thought of your anointed hands laid on me. I pray and hope I am one of your heirs that keeps you proud to carry the family legacy continually.

To my Sims family...I love you to life. Thank you for encouraging me to keep the love brand new every time we see each other.

To my Hall Family...Let's keep the passion and love going forever and ever. Our ancestors are depending on us.

To my tailored coaches - Laura Bulluck, Tina Brown, Brian Harris, Tim and Teri Vaughan, Dana Franklin, Veronica Calloway, Drs. Bryant & Deborah Robinson - the coach I am today, is because of the coach you've always been to and for me over the years. Whether the season is dark or light, victorious or laborious, you've proven the mandate is truly placed you.

To my writing coach... author, Keena C. Rimson - thanks for taking the assignment and journey to punch me into my self-publication since 2013. Your spirit of humility and exhortation makes it easy to flow and go! It has taken me years to get here, my friend, now your watering will give God the increase. The world is waiting for you!

My Author's Circle- Dr. Edmond Kelly, Tina Brown, Laura C. Bulluck, Keena C. Rimson, and Darryl L. Rivers - your hunger to write to the world stirred me to not only be there for you but take you everywhere I can be. Thank you for trusting me with your book birthings and your allowances to share the same stages. This is OUR legacy!

Pastor Samuel Giles (Life Center Ministries Family) & Pastor Sidney B. Ford (Pleasant Grove Baptist Church Family) of Georgia ... your mentorship, pastoral care, service to my family created an anointed sound of honor through love during a season of construction and growing pains in ways I could never forget. THANK YOU!

Bishop Rory R. Marshall, Sr. (Nehemiah Urban Church Ministries Family) Chicago, Illinois...since my 2004 ordination, this book title, and rhema word was birthed and now resurrected to bless the masses in a national publication. Thank you for your forever mentorship, prayer, and support in various levels of ministry and entrepreneurial achievements. I am grateful to be a spiritual son!

To all whom I fail or simply forgot to write your name, please allow me to make mention of you as I service you in the volume pages of this book. With renewed faith and the fifteen years of strength it has taken to produce this publication, know that I love You, I'm praying for You, and I hope that is what matters most.

ABOUT THE AUTHOR

A native Chicagoan, Dr. Sims began his career as an interim educator, teen mentor, and behavior interventionist. In 2013, Dr. Sims followed his passions to launched several entrepreneurial ventures that awarded him success in organizational leadership, national sales teams, and in the barber and beauty cultural industry in the southwest region of Arizona. Dr. Sims has produced two self-publication books titled, "Speechless Conversations -"A Poetic Style of Life Lessons & Perspectives" in 2014 and "Quotes on Napkins-Snacks of Inspiration for the Heart & Soul" in 2016. You can order both publications:

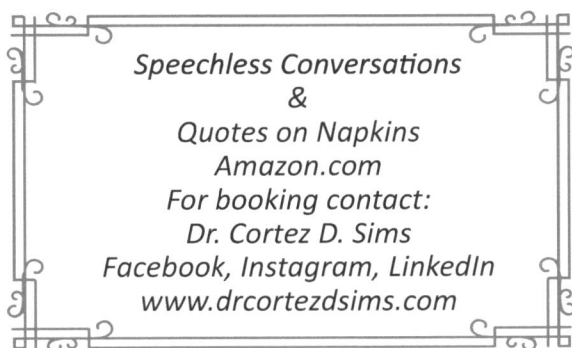

Speechless Conversations
&
Quotes on Napkins
Amazon.com
For booking contact:
Dr. Cortez D. Sims
Facebook, Instagram, LinkedIn
www.drcortezdsims.com

www.ingramcontent.com/pod-product-compliance
Lightning Source LLC
Chambersburg PA
CBHW041623110426
42740CB00042BA/35